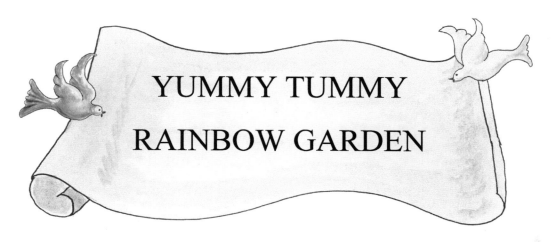

YUMMY TUMMY
RAINBOW GARDEN

The beginning of a healthy life for all girls and boys

by

Karen Leonetti, CDA, CDS
Child Development Specialist

Illustrated by

Lee Libro

ISBN 978-0615836928

Earth Angels Publishing

Printed in the U.S.A.

The e-book version of this product should be considered a living document and I reserve the right to edit, update and improve upon it at any time.

"Karen has creatively written a much needed nutritional storybook for families to read together. Her book is a fun adventure of the senses for her readers, teaching the delicious beauty of fresh garden foods and how they keep us Fit for Life. She understands the nation's high obesity rates and wants to share her book, teaching fresh Grow-Food benefits and encouraging healthy outdoor time and eating well. She has captured this in a story portraying cooperation and determination in exploring for their Rainbow Garden outside adventure. I love how her story begins and ends with a pair of friendly birds helping her characters find and then share the fresh food knowledge she has written, paying it forward."

—*Harvey Diamond*
"Fit for Life"

"Children, their parents and teachers will enjoy this educational story with a heart— that encourages kids to find real treasure! This "magical" book takes children on a self-guided adventure that is fun, nutritious and delicious."

—*Amy Dickinson,*
Nationally Syndicated "Ask Amy" Advice Columnist

"An amazing story, transporting us on a nutritious journey energizing everyone with the importance of healthy living. Karen recognizes the vital connections to nature and life-long attributes of eating from the Earth!"

—Dr. Michelle Summers,
Childhood Educator Professor
University of South Florida

"Karen's message is perfect! Teaching children at a young age to get outside in the sun and exercise away from the computer and Xbox and TV! I like the rainbow correlation with the colorful fruits and vegetables"

—Dr. Michael Lange
Board Certified Optometric Physician and Certified Nutrition Specialist
and Syndicated Talk Show Host of "Ask the Dr."

Forward

With childhood obesity at an all-time high, Karen is excited to write her fun and educational children's book for both children and adults alike. She lovingly shares child-approved and taste-tested healthy recipes of her own at the back of this book. She understands that a healthy life begins in the home kitchen by preparing fun, nutritious foods together for a healthy family food bond that lasts a lifetime. Table-time as a family is priceless and extremely necessary in this high-tech time we all live in. She suggests eating together as a family (at the table) at least three nights a week. Buying fresh organic Grow-Foods isn't costly. Expensive foods tend to be the factory prepackaged, processed foods full of harmful food dyes and chemicals. A bag of apples costs around $4.99 and a bag of chips costs about the same. The apples last MUCH longer and are packed with vitamins and minerals too. She encourages families to spend more money on organic foods that will result in healthier bodies. If organic food is not available, try to select produce free of chemical pesticides. Fresh food is preventative medicine. Better yet, grow your own food.

In the back of this book are easy, fun recipes to make together. Time shared in the kitchen creates future memories of healthy goodness!

Please NOTE: If you involve your children in the healthy food purchasing and preparing, they will most likely try it. Offer "Taste Tests" over at least a two week period. Removing sugary snacks and candy for two weeks allows the taste buds to appreciate the fresh food flavors and goodness, also reducing sugar cravings.

This book has been carefully sown, watered and nurtured with love. It is now time for your family to reap the bounties of her harvest and YOURS. Enjoy!

Finally, I am not claiming to be a nutritionist. Any food choices remain the parent's decision. I am solely providing a storybook for children to assist them to "Eat Well" through a fun gardening adventure.

Dedication

Few authors dedicate a book to themselves, but this is one of them. My health-depleted body boomeranged back to total health through organic, fresh "Grow-Foods." I thank my dad, Dick Wilsen, for providing my first garden plot at age four. To my mom, who always encouraged "Taste Tests" and for lovingly nurturing her family with what was best for them and not wavering from fresh food choices on the table. To my amazing husband, Danny, who helped me to survive, has allowed me to always taste the joys in life, to sow the seeds of happiness and to be "naturally particular." To my first editor, Suzi Harkola, who helped me to get my words into the computer at the beginning of my writing adventure. To Lee Libro, who assisted and encouraged me to complete edits along with creating my beautiful watercolor illustrations. To all my family and many lovingly supportive friends who understand my quirkiness and love to learn with me along the journey. Lastly, I give thanks to my mom, Wanda Wilsen, for the final hours of editing together sitting side by side, pen in hand. I love and thank you all for your support!

Once upon a time there were two friends named Earth and Angel. Sadly, they stayed inside almost every day.

One day, they became bored watching TV and playing video games. They noticed that their bodies felt slow and lethargic, so they decided to go OUTSIDE for an adventure.

"Let's go outside and play! Hip, hip hooray!"

As they opened the door, two sweetly singing birds swooped down and gave them a rolled up paper. It felt MAGICAL!

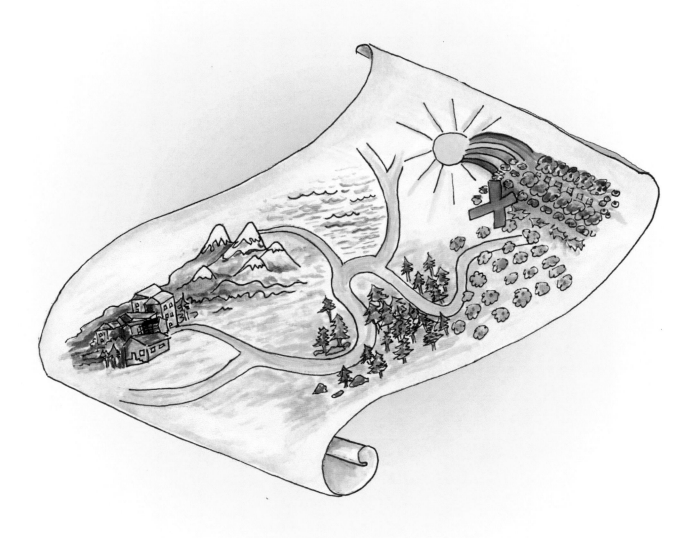

"Oooh, it's a TREASURE MAP!" said Earth. "There by the red X it looks like a Yummy Tummy Rainbow Garden."

"Let's follow our map and see if we can find this garden," said Angel. They noticed it felt great to be outside.

As they began following their map, a rain cloud rolled in and gentle raindrops fell down upon their heads. The rain felt so refreshing.

The children danced and sang in the rain. It was so much fun!

Don't give up searching.
It is always closer than you think.

Soon they were tired and hungry. They wanted to go back home.

"Don't give up searching; it is always closer than you think," the wind gently whispered to them.

After the rain had stopped, Earth and Angel could SMELL how fresh the air was. This reminded them about eating fresh foods that grow so brightly in a garden.

"Let's call it "Grow-Food!" They both smiled just thinking about all the freshly grown food.

"But where can we find it?" asked Angel.

"Follow your treasure map and don't give up. You KNOW you can find it," whispered the whistling wind.

"We WILL find fresh food growing in a garden that will make us grow stronger. Not like food from a package, box or can."

Earth and Angel looked up and saw a colorful
rainbow stretching across the sky.

It looked just like the rainbow on their treasure map.

"Wouldn't it be FUN to taste all the colors of that rainbow?" said Earth.

"I bet they would taste delicious," said Angel. "Do you think they would be sweet, sour, crunchy or juicy?"

Then they noticed lovely orange trees on their map, by the red X, and just ahead there they were!

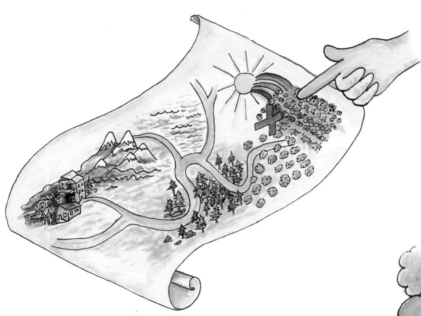

They ran to the orange grove and climbed the ladder by the nearest tree. They climbed to the very top. And what do you think they saw?

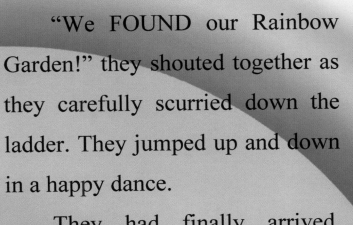

"We FOUND our Rainbow Garden!" they shouted together as they carefully scurried down the ladder. They jumped up and down in a happy dance.

They had finally arrived. They had NOT given up! They were ready to taste the colorful "Grow-Foods" growing in the garden.

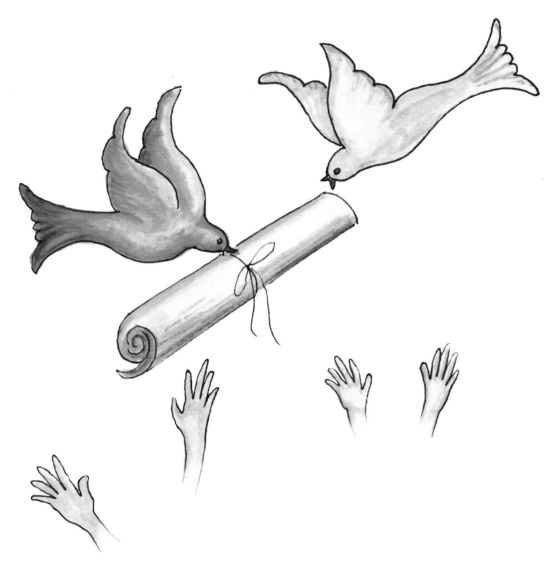

They smiled and carefully rolled up the map. Hearing the same sweetly singing birds, they held the map high over their heads. The birds swooped down to pick up and deliver the map to yet another family needing to learn about healthy foods.

As they entered the garden, they noticed a sign that read:

Welcome to your
Yummy Tummy Rainbow Garden.
We are happy you found us.
Pick and eat whatever you wish and
PLEASE remember to water us
before you leave.

They noticed that some food grows on trees, such as the mango, orange and starfruit.

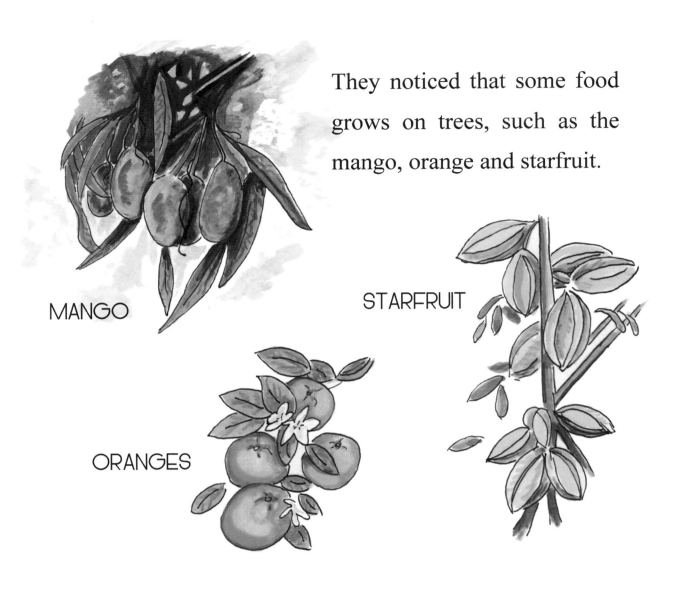

MANGO

STARFRUIT

ORANGES

And some of their favorite vegetables grow under the ground such as carrots, beets and potatoes.

They found celery stalks, green spinach, red juicy tomatoes and crunchy purple cabbages and even sprawling strawberry plants.

Bushes held sweet blueberries, vines dangled clusters of grapes and trees grew bunches of bananas or sour lemons.

EVERY COLOR OF THE RAINBOW!

It is fun to eat food picked fresh from the garden outside instead of foods made inside a factory or ordered from a drive-up window.

"Shall we start eating? I am hungry!" said Angel.

"YES," said Earth. As they looked closer they saw special signs by each row explaining how each food helps their bodies.

Welcome to your
Yummy Tummy Rainbow Garden
We are happy you found us.
Pick and eat whatever you wish and
PLEASE remember to water us
before you leave.

The first sign said:

Tomato, tomato, what do you do? I have four chambers inside me, just like your heart. I help it pump healthy blood through your veins, that's what I do.

The second sign said:

Beets, beets, what do you do? I am red like your blood and I clean your blood too.

The third sign said:

Carrots, carrots what do you do? When you slice me I look like your eyes, so I help you to see better in the day and at nighttime, too.

The next sign read:

Yellow banana, yellow banana, what do you do? I hang in bunches from a tree. I am good for a cough and sooth your throat, too.

Green celery was next:

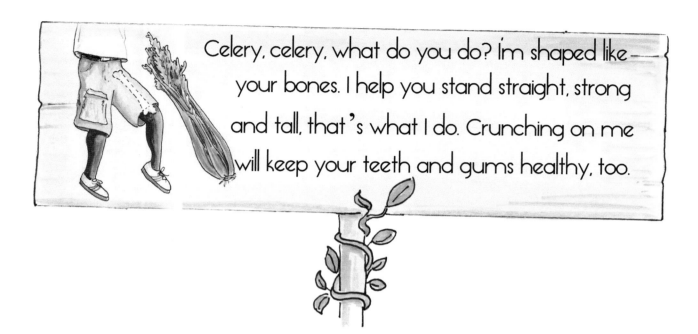

Celery, celery, what do you do? I'm shaped like your bones. I help you stand straight, strong and tall, that's what I do. Crunching on me will keep your teeth and gums healthy, too.

Blueberries on bushes were next:

Blueberry, blueberry, what do you do? I am good for your memory so you can learn faster and remember more, too.

Next was purple cabbage:

There was also a special walnut tree in this Yummy Tummy Garden. Its sign said:

The last sign showed:

Did you know that orange-colored foods like carrots, oranges, apricot, mango, peaches, cantaloupe, pumpkin, sweet potatoes, squash, and peppers, too, can help your eyes see better for you?

As Earth and Angel were tasting, munching and snacking on their fresh fun foods; they noticed something exciting happening inside their OWN bodies! "ZING, ZAM, ZEE, these foods are GREAT for me!"

SHAZAM! Just like magic, their tummies were filled with great nutrients from nature's fruits, veggies, nuts and seeds. They felt healthy and happy to have learned more about "Grow-Foods" too. "Delicious and nutritious!" they both shouted.

Earth & Angel learned that freshly grown foods do not have chemicals and dyes such as red #40, blue #1 and yellow #5 that are harmful for our brain and the rest of our body.

When we eat fresh "Grow-Foods" we feel healthy, strong and FAST. Some even taste like nature's candy.

"Fresh fruits and veggies give us ZIPPY vitamins and MONSTER minerals," they said proudly.

Tell all your friends, so they can be faster and smarter too.

After they finished eating, their tummies felt satisfied and happy. Not too much and not too little, JUST RIGHT!

Looking around for a trash can for their peels and pits, they heard the garden say, "Feed me your peels and pits and I will decompose them back into garden soil." They gently laid them in a compost pile, as the garden said.

Earth and Angel were THRILLED with their adventure.

Now they knew how healthy foods taste and look. They were excited to share with friends, family, neighbors and teachers at school what they had learned.

"We can even plant our own backyard garden or join in a community garden."

"We can even make our own HEALTHY juices and smoothies using fresh fruits such as, apples, kale and bananas," they giggled.

Before they left the garden, they remembered the first sign. Do you remember what they were supposed to do?

They discovered that magical watering can which mysteriously was always kept full.

YES, they did remember, and happily watered the plants to keep THEM healthy and growing bigger and stronger... like YOU!

Earth and Angel now LOVE exercising EVERY day such as jumping, skateboarding, biking, hiking and gardening, too. At least sixty minutes of outside exercise will do.

Remember… always eat a rainbow EVERY day. Fresh fruits, veggies, raw nuts and seeds too. The animals eat them and so should YOU! They are delicious and NUTRITIOUS!

"Thank you for coming on this adventure with us out in the healthy fresh air and trees, for more GREEN time outside and less SCREEN time inside in front of a T.V. or computer," chirped the birds, happily.

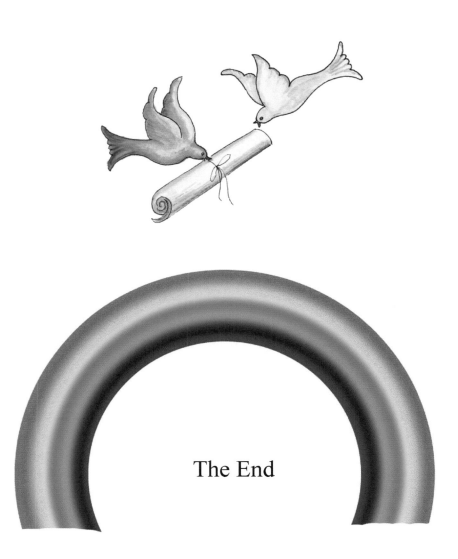

The End

Recipes, Notes & Hints

1. Children love sweets! The following hand-picked selection is a healthy sugar snack/ dessert alternative delivering a powerful punch of vitamins, minerals and healthy fats for optimum brain development!

2. If your child is used to consuming sugar sweetened snacks, be patient with these recipes. It may take up to 2-4 weeks for their "Sweet-Tooth Palette" to change to enjoy naturally sweetened GOODNESS.

3. Brush teeth after eating dates or dried fruit as they contain sticky sugar coating that gets in between teeth. They can also rinse mouth by swishing water.

4. Be positive with your child while preparing food together.

5. Don't expect a problem getting them to eat well.

6. If need be, any of the recipes can be sweetened naturally by adding more:

    Maple Syrup
    Agave
    Honey
    Black Strap Molasses
    Dates

As sweet taste buds shift from undesirable sugar or artificial sweeteners, you can slowly reduce natural sweeteners, too, to enjoy the real taste of the Fresh Food Goodness.

Remember to be patient and keep creating these healthy recipes over and over again together. It is the process that creates memories!

May these healthy snack treats created as a family together,
Be Yummy in your Tummy!
ENJOY!

Sources

Most ingredients can be purchased on my blog: FreshFood4Kids.com

Click on the Natural Zing box to order recipe ingredients or power mixer from my website.

For essential oils such as:
Peppermint, wild orange, ginger, spearmint, tangerine, basil, lemon, etc.
Please visit my essential oil website: www.mydoterra.com/Leonetti

Only use therapeutic grade essential oils for food creations to enhance recipes and health.

GREEN Swamp Monster Smoothie©

An easy, good base for all smoothies. Create your own too!

Ingredients
1 cup water (filtered), coconut water or coconut or almond milk
1-2 tablespoons chia seeds (omega and protein)
3-4 frozen bananas*
1-2 cups kale, spinach or other dark green leafy greens (fresh picked or frozen)
1-2 tablespoons coconut oil or olive oil (Oil helps the body absorb calcium from greens.)

Preparation
*Peel, then break or cut bananas in half. Lay flat in single layer in plastic baggie in freezer, if possible on tray or flat surface. Can use unfrozen bananas also, just add some ice cubes to chill.
In blender carafe, add water, chia seeds, bananas, oil and greens.
Mix until smooth and enjoy together with a SMILE.

Try adding: Any fruit or berries (fresh or frozen) avocado, sunflower or peanut butter, flax, sunflower seeds, almonds, hemp hearts or other shelled nuts or seeds to your liking.

To sweeten, add: 1-4 PITTED dates, ¼ cup honey, maple syrup or agave. As your family gets used to less sugar, try to "Amp Up" the greens and use less bananas and sweetener.

(See my websites, FreshFood4Kids.com and www.mydoterra.com/Leonetti to purchase ingredients for recipes.)

Earth & Angel's No-Bake Treats©
I have fond memories of making these with my grandmother.
Here is a healthier version.

Ingredients
1 cup maple syrup (grade B has more minerals)
2 teaspoons pure vanilla extract
2 teaspoons soft or melted (low heat) coconut oil
1 teaspoon sea salt (Celtic preferred for maximum minerals)
3 cups rolled oats (For gluten free, use Bob's Red Mill Oaks marked gluten free)
Optional: unsweetened coconut flakes or any chopped seeds to roll balls in (kids love this)

Preparation
Mix above in medium size bowl. Then add ingredients below and stir well.

1 cup almond, sunflower or peanut butter (plain or crunchy)
½ cup raw cacao powder (or cocoa powder)

By hand, pinch walnut size piece, roll into balls or flatten like a cookie.
Dust with coconut flakes or roll in cocoa powder or any chopped seeds.*
Can also scoop with spoon and drop mounded onto tray.
Put in freezer for 30 minutes to "set", longer to harden.
Place in container and store in fridge or freezer for healthy "Grab & Go" snacks.
Try adding for additional protein: 1 tablespoon: * chia, sesame, ground flax seed, chopped nuts, coconut flakes for variety of goodness.

(See my websites, FreshFood4Kids.com and www.mydoterra.com/Leonetti to purchase ingredients for recipes.)

Mother Earth Raw Pudding Mousse ©

Ingredients
¾ cup raw cacao powder or cocoa powder
½ cup coconut oil
¾ cup maple syrup (preferably grade B, more mineral dense)
1 tablespoons PURE vanilla (to taste)
1/2 teaspoon Celtic or sea salt
3-4 cups firmly packed (6-7 small) avocado~ peeled, pitted, scooped~ Fresh or
frozen

Preparation
Peel, scoop avocado. (Being careful to discard small hard stem piece of avocado
when scooping. Blend all together until super smooth & rich in *high speed mixer.
Note~ Avocado can be scooped and frozen to last for months in baggie or Mason jar
(Leave space at the top for expansion when freezing in Mason jar)

Add one drop of doTERRA* peppermint or orange food grade pure essential oil for
a chocolate mint pick-me-up treat! Cover in fridge. Mousse will harden a bit due to
coconut oil. Can be frozen in Popsicle molds if it doesn't get devoured immediately.

(See my websites, FreshFood4Kids.com and www.mydoterra.com/Leonetti to
purchase ingredients for recipes.)

Nuts about Banana Splits©

Ingredients
1 ripe banana (one per person)
2 tablespoons sunflower, cashew, almond or peanut butter

Toppings of choice
Goji berries, raisins, coconut flakes, cacao nibs, sunflower seeds.
Chopped walnuts, chia seeds, sliced almonds, etc.

Preparation
Gently cut banana almost all the way through
Smear nut butter inside split banana gently with butter knife or spoon
Generously sprinkle with above toppings of choice
Squeeze together and pick up to eat or cut with fork & knife to eat, teaching your child cutting skills
Wrap for child's lunch box or storage container…nutritious YUMMY in their Tummy!

(See my websites, FreshFood4Kids.com and www.mydoterra.com/Leonetti to purchase ingredients for recipes.)

Recipe Photography Credits:
Lynn Morris at www.LynnsLens.com Sarasota, Florida

.

About the Author

Karen Leonetti and her adoring husband, Danny, relocated to Black Mountain, North Carolina after having lived in a 1950 cottage on Siesta Key in Sarasota, Florida since 1984. She is a proud cancer survivor-thriver since 1994 of Non-Hodgkin's Lymphoma cancer as a result of pesticide exposure. After her survival of an autologous bone marrow transplant at Moffitt Cancer Hospital and her healing protocol of chemo and radiation to her heart area, Karen and Danny decided to open an eco-green preschool in 1996, naming it appropriately "Earth Angel Preschool." Their passionate mission is to teach the fun of eating healthy fruits, veggies, seeds and nuts. They teach throughout the country about the benefits of eating smarter for optimum health. They also strive to have families create together a backyard organic garden. Karen and Danny also enjoy teaching classes and sharing unique fun ways to get "Kiddos jazzed " about preparing, tasting and eating fresh foods. They demo spiraling their veggies into fun zucchini "pasta" and ribbon curls from various produce. Karen has been a speaker for her local Holistic Mom's Network and Whole Foods Market as their Green Kids Club monthly presenter. Teaching at a local Elementary school for "Fun Fresh Food Friday" was a monthly highlight.

Karen has had several articles published on positive child development and parenting. In addition, she teaches children's hands-on etiquette classes to help nurture their spirit and makes our world a more well- mannered pleasant planet. She is a member of Slow Food USA, Holistic Moms Network and Prevent Obesity. She also enjoys coaching parents to live in harmony with their children.

To contact Karen & Danny please go to:
FreshFood4Kids@gmail.com
FreshFood4Kids.com   Blog
Yummy Tummy Rainbow Garden   FB
Please post photos of your family working in your veggie garden, large or small, on our FB book page.

About the Illustrator

Lee Libro is a published author, book designer and artist. Her illustration work ranges from realistic watercolors to visionary paintings inspired by dreams and her passion for literary themes and symbols. Having worked for twenty years in Advertising and Marketing Communications with a degree in English, she is now enjoying self-made abundance following her first love as an artist. She is the proud mother of five grown children and now resides in Lakewood Ranch, Florida with her husband and two dogs.

Visit Lee Libro's websites:

LeeLibro.imagekind.com
www.smilingbuddhaboutique.com
www.literary-magic.com

or contact her at TheQuillGuild@aol.com

Made in the USA
Charleston, SC
08 February 2014